Brera

D0129336

Brief Guide

Brera

edited by Stefano Zuffi

Brief Guide

Electa

Cover illustration
Raphael,
The Marriage of the Virgin, detail.
Milan, Pinacoteca di Brera

Translation by Christine Mac Lellan
for *Scriptum*, Rome

This volume was published by Electa, Milan
Elemond Editori Associati

Contents

Introduction

The Pinacoteca di Brera is two hundred years old, its history dating from 1799 with the arrival of the first group of paintings, four altarpieces from the church of Santi Cosma e Damiano alla Scala in Milan. In the years that followed there was much activity: requisitions, acquisitions, exchanges, and radical changes in the architecture of the building (including the almost total destruction of a fourteenth-century church), all contributed to the rapid expansion of the collection and its transformation into a fine Napoleonic museum, a fact borne out by the bronze statue of Napoleon by Canova that stands in the centre of the majestic baroque courtyard. Its vast rooms with their palatial neoclassical feel house an imposing collection of paintings including a large number of altarpieces. Most of the works are from Lombardy, Veneto, Romagna and the Marche (the areas Bonaparte conquered), although no sooner had these arrived than great efforts were made to obtain examples of painting from other regions as well as from abroad, to try to offer the public as wide a range as possible, so that they could gain an understanding of the evolution of painting between the fifteenth and eighteenth centuries. According to the tastes of the time, earlier painting tended to be undervalued and considered "primitive," although this gap was remedied at least in part later on. Only a part of the Brera collection was displayed in the rooms of the museum: many of the larger works were loaned out to decorate the churches of Milan and surroundings; some were destined to become showpieces in public buildings; others ended up in store rooms. And so the Brera collection became known as the dispersed collection, and has only now been fully registered as a result of recent cataloguing projects, much research, study and evaluation.

Throughout much of the nineteenth century, the Pinacoteca existed alongside the Accademia di Belle Arti, forming a sort of annex, and providing a collection of models from the past on which the art students could practise. In 1882, the two institutions became independent and since then the Pinacoteca has lost its original instructive and celebratory function. Acquisitions were carefully chosen (often with

Orazio Gentileschi,
The Martyrs Valerian, Tiburtius and Cecilia Visited by an Angel,
detail.
Milan, Pinacoteca di Brera

help from the eminent Associazione Amici di Brera, the Friends of Brera) and improvements constantly made to how the works were displayed until Brera became synonymous with a dynamic, constantly changing museum. The damage during the Second World War, when much of the museum was destroyed by incendiary bombs, forced the authorities into a further phase of rethinking that led to the formulation of the project that became known as the "Grande Brera" launched by Franco Russoli in the seventies. A series of technical and structural problems have had to be dealt with to reach the final stages of this objective. The uninterrupted sequence of acquisitions, which are also of a very high standard, the steady reorganization of the exhibition space, and the inauguration of new areas have restored Brera to its former role as a museum of prestige and international standing, and an artistic and cultural reference point.

This brief guide to the Pinacoteca di Brera gathers together the museum's most famous paintings and describes them in chronological order.

The Rooms

Room I
Jesi Donation: twentieth-century painting and sculpture

Room IA
Mocchirolo Chapel

Rooms II, III, IV
Italian painting from the thirteenth to the sixteenth century

Room V
Fifteenth and sixteenth century Venetian painting

Room VI
Fifteenth and sixteenth century Venetian painting

Room VII
Sixteenth century Venetian portraits

Room VIII
Fifteenth century Venetian painting

Room IX
Sixteenth century Venetian painting

Room XIV
Sixteenth century Venetian painting

Room XV
Fifteenth and sixteenth century Lombard paintings and frescoes

Room XVIII
Sixteenth century Lombard paintings

Room XIX
Fifteenth and sixteenth century Lombard portraits and sacred art

Room XX
Fifteenth century paintings of Emilia and Ferrara

Room XXI
Fifteenth-century polyptychs from the Marche

Room XXII
Fifteenth- and sixteenth-century paintings of Emilia and Ferrara

Room XXIII
Sixteenth-century paintings of Emilia and Ferrara

Room XXIV
Piero della Francesca, Signorelli, Bramante, Raphael

Room XXVII
Fifteenth- and sixteenth-century painting in central Italy

Room XXVIII
Seventeenth-century painting in central Italy

Room XXIX
Caravaggio and the Caravaggeschi

Room XXX
Seventeenth century Lombard painting

Room XXXI
Seventeenth century Italian and Flemish paintings

Rooms XXXII, XXXIII
Sixteenth and seventeenth century Dutch and Flemish paintings

Room XXXIV
Eighteenth century sacred art

Rooms XXXV, XXXVI
Eighteenth century Venetian paintings, genre paintings and Italian portraits

Rooms XXXVII, XXXVIII
Nineteenth century Italian paintings

List of the artists

Andrea Appiani
59 *Olympus (Coronation of Jupiter)*

Federico Barocci
37 *Martyrdom of St Vitalis*

Evaristo Baschenis
49 *Still Life with Musical Instruments*

Jacopo Bassano (Jacopo da Ponte)
35 *St Roch Visits the Plague Victims*

Gentile Bellini and Giovanni Bellini
19 *St Mark Preaching in Alexandria*

Giovanni Bellini
21 *Madonna and Child*

Bernardo Bellotto
55 *View of Villa Melzi alla Gazzada*
View of Gazzada

Bergognone (Ambrogio da Fossano)
9 *Madonna and Child, St Catherine of Siena and a Carthusian Monk*

Umberto Boccioni
65 *Riot in the Galleria*

Bonifacio Veronese (Bonifazio de' Pitati)
31 *Moses Rescued from the Water*

Paris Bordon
29 *Holy Family with St Ambrose and Donor*

Donato Bramante
15 *Christ at the Column*

Bramantino (Bartolomeo Suardi)
16 *Crucifixion*

Vincenzo Campi
38 *Fruit Seller*

Canaletto (Giovanni Antonio Canal)
54 *View of the Basin of San Marco from the Customs Point*
View of the Grand Canal Looking Towards the Customs Point, from Campo San Vio

Caravaggio (Michelangelo Merisi)
41 *Supper at Emmaus*

Vittore Carpaccio
22 *St Stephen's Dispute with the Doctors of the Sanhedrin*

The Master of Mocchirolo

active in Lombardy in the second
half of the fourteenth century

2 *The Porro Oratory
of Mocchirolo*

frescoes transferred to canvas

This room was set up in 1949
specifically to house the large parts
of the frescoes that had survived

from the oratory of Santa Caterina
in Mocchirolo, near Lentate
(Milan). Commissioned by the
Porro family (the coat of arms
with leeks on a field of red
and yellow stripes appears in
several places along the edges)
and painted around 1370,
the frescoes are the work by an
anonymous painter influenced by
Giovanni da Milano, and can be
counted among the most

important examples of Lombard
painting in the fourteenth
century. The calmness of line,
gesture and feeling that links
them with Tuscan painting
and Giotto's sojourn in Milan
in the fourth decade of the
thirteenth century, is enriched
by the pink colour and the
accurate loving reproduction
of realistic detail typical of the
Lombard tradition.

13

Giovanni da Milano

Caversaccio, Como,
recorded 1346-1369

3 *Christ Enthroned
Adored by Angels*

tempera on panel,
152.3 × 68.5 cm

The Black Death of 1348 had
a profound effect on European
art and culture. The return
to archaic severity in Tuscan
paintings in the second half
of the fourteenth century is
borne witness to by the seminal
Christ in Judgement, painted in
Florence by Giovanni da Milano
(he actually came from the
province of Como), one of the
most important post-Giotto
painters. It was most probably
the central panel of a polyptych
commissioned between 1360
and 1365 from the monastery
of Santa Maria degli Angeli, now
dispersed in various museums.
The panel is in a good state of
conservation. The figure of Christ
sits face on, unperturbable
and solidly seated on a throne
decorated with lions' heads. He is
flanked by four angels in profile
who seem almost frightened
in the face of the energy of the
supreme Judge.

Gentile da Fabriano

Fabriano, Ancona,
1385 ca - Rome 1427

④ *The Valle Romita Polyptych*

tempera on panel
central panel 157.2 × 79.6 cm;
lower side panels 117.5 × 40 cm;
upper side panels 48.9 × 37.8 cm
signed bottom centre
of the central panel:

"gentilis de fabriano pinxit"

An early masterpiece by the
most influential artist of the first
quarter of the fifteenth century,
the polyptych dates from
approximately 1410. It came
to Brera from the monastery of
Valle Romita, close to Fabriano,
in the Marches, but it is not
possible to reconstruct the
original aspect of the group.

The panels of the polyptych,
mounted in a Neo-Gothic early
nineteenth-century frame, hold
a complete collection
of the subjects common to
International Gothic: the large
central scene with the *Coronation
of the Virgin* seems to shimmer
in the rich shiny gold of the
celestial background, while the
figures are clothed in wonderfully
elegant flowing robes.

15

Girolamo di Giovanni

Camerino, recorded
1449-1474

5 *The Gualdo Tadino Polyptych*

tempera on panel
lower central panel, 132 × 60 cm;
lower side panels, 118 × 42 cm
upper central panel, 190 × 60 cm;
upper side panels, 154 × 42 cm

(in storage from the Poldi Pezzoli
Museum)

This polyptych, the upper order
of which came to Brera from the
cathedral of Gualdo Tadino, dates
from about 1462. It is the work of
Girolamo di Giovanni, the principal
exponent of the school of painting
that arose in the fifteenth century
in Camerino. Although apparently
limited to his "provincial"

boundaries, as the use of the
gold background would suggest,
Girolamo was in fact well versed
in the techniques of the day. A
visit to Padua in circa 1450 put
him in touch with Donatello and
Mantegna. But above all, Girolamo
di Giovanni was one of the first
artists to pick up on Piero della
Francesca's work and translate it
to great effect into the figurative
language of the polyptych.

Piero della Francesca

Sansepolcro, Arezzo,
1415/1420-1492

6 *The Montefeltro Altarpiece*

tempera and oil on panel,
251 × 172 cm

Painted between 1472 and 1474
for Duke Federico da Montefeltro,
this altarpiece was originally
created for the church of San
Bernardino in Urbino. The two
creative impulses of Piero della
Francesca come together in this
work: one, his fascination with
geometry (he wrote two fundamental
treatises on perspective); and two,
the creative artist in search of the
ideal image. The scene is set inside
a Renaissance building, the
proportions of which have been
carefully calculated in relation to
the figures. There is a quality
of brightness, of silence, about
the light that falls on the figures
that seems to give the exalted
tone of a celestial court. The
ostrich egg is a famous detail,
in which the symbolic value
(alluding to the birth of Jesus
and the heraldic device of the
Montefeltro) is combined with
an impressive demonstration of
how to give depth to the scene.

Francesco del Cossa

Ferrara 1436 ca - Bologna 1478

7 *Saint John the Baptist*
Saint Peter

tempera on panel,
112 × 55 cm each

The side panels of the *Griffoni Polyptych*, painted by Francesco del Cossa in 1473 for the basilica of San Petronio in Bologna, other panels of which are to be found in the museums of Rome, London and Washington, are among the most prized pieces in the Brera collection. The two figures, statuesque and vigorous, are in an excellent state of conservation. They stand out against a compact dense blue sky that gives them a very clear outline. The details in the features of the saints and the minute landscapes reveal the influence of Flemish painting, while the classical feel and keen interest in perspective suggest the highly advanced humanistic culture of Ferrara, where reference to Rogier van der Weyden was combined with the study of Leon Battista Alberti.

Ercole de' Roberti

Ferrara 1450 ca-1496

⑧ *The Santa Maria in Porto Altarpiece*

oil on canvas, 323 × 240 cm

This altarpiece, executed in 1480 for the church of Santa Maria in Porto in Ravenna, is one of the greatest compositions of Ercole de' Roberti, who is here attempting to achieve a balance between the typical characters of the Ferrarese school and the compositional monumentality of Tuscan art. In the vast expanse of the canvas, the few and imposing figures have been modelled with a robustness that gives them the appearance of statues. A characteristic element is the Virgin's throne, which is raised on a plinth decorated with bas reliefs. The podium has been raised up by a circle of small polychrome pillars thus creating space for an evocative glimpse of a seascape. Created according to strict geometric rules, with its thin stiff figures, the altarpiece becomes a sort of a sacred apparition.

**Bergognone
(Ambrogio da Fossano)**

Milan? 1453 ca - Milan 1523

9 *Madonna and Child,
Saint Catherine of Siena
and a Carthusian Monk*

tempera on panel, 46 × 40.5 cm

This small panel was probably
originally created to decorate one
of the monks' cells in the Certosa
of Pavia, for which Bergognone
had completed frescoes and
panels on a number of occasions.
It bears all the marks of
Bergognone's early years of work
in the monastery, such as the use
of a terse limpid light that
outlines the forms, the careful

execution of the portrait of the
monk in the foreground and
above all the beautiful landscape
in the background, where every
single detail is imbued with a
typically Lombard atmosphere
of calm tinged with melancholy.

Vincenzo Foppa

Brescia 1472 ca - 1515 ca

10 *The Grazie Polyptych*

tempera and oil on panel
central panels: lower section
Madonna and Child with Angels,
185.5 × 98.5 cm; upper section:
*Saint Francis Receiving
the Stigmata*, 144 × 96.5 cm

The original frame for this
polyptych from the church
of Santa Maria delle Grazie,
in Bergamo, is unfortunately
missing, making it difficult
to recreate the overall effect.
Nevertheless, this group of panels
suggests an organic and single
architectural structure, with
a portico at ground level and
a loggia on the upper floor;
the floor on which the saints

stand is seen in perspective.
*Saint Francis Receiving the
Stigmata*, at the centre of the
upper panel, is set in the country
near the monastery; the main
scene with the Madonna
enthroned, is, in contrast, set
within a vault with a very deep
perspective, but the unusual
gesture of the Child plucking the
strings of an angel's lute breaks
the rigour of the form.

Carlo Crivelli

Venice 1430 ca -
 Marche 1494/1495

⓫ *The Madonna of the Candle*

oil on panel, 218 × 75 cm
signed under the throne:
"KAROLVS CRIVELLUS VENETVS
EQVES LAVREATVS PINXIT"

Born and trained in Veneto,
Crivelli studied in Padua with
Mantegna, Cosmè Tura, Foppa
and other noteworthy masters of
northern Italy. He thus received
a thorough grounding in the
study of perspective before
deciding to leave the Veneto
region for the Marche, where
he was to live out his life
as a painter. In a context that was
still partly bound up with a high
Gothic culture, Crivelli mixed
modern solutions with traditional
overlays (such as the gold
background or the insertion
of details in relief). The result
is often fascinating, as the many
works in the Pinacoteca di Brera
demonstrate, such as the
Camerino polyptych, now
dispersed (1490), of which
the elongated richly embellished
Madonna of the Candle was part,
and where the exuberant wealth
of decoration seems to stop short
before the melancholy face of the
Virgin.

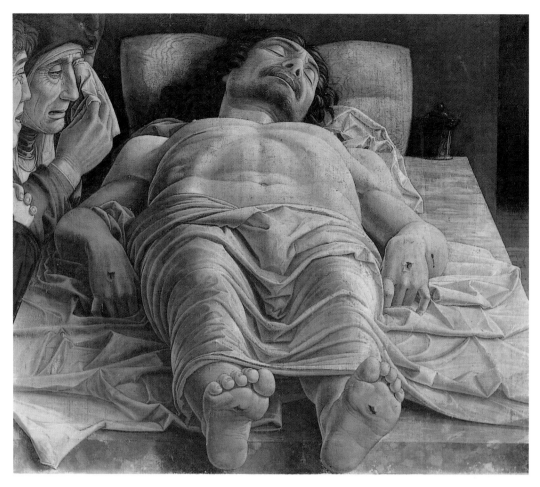

Andrea Mantegna

Isola di Carturo, Padua,
1430 ca - Mantua 1506

12 *Lamentation over
the Dead Christ*

tempera on canvas, 68 × 81 cm

This masterful work of art was
probably painted by Mantegna
towards the end of his life
for his own tomb in the church
of Sant'Andrea in Mantua.

It is a highly experimental
work from both a technical
and compositional point
of view. Technically it is
one of the rare works on
canvas of the period, while
the composition has been
given a steeply invasive,
almost obsessive, foreshortened
perspective. The body of Christ,
laid out on the cold slab
of a dark morgue, is depicted
in the gelid immobility of death,
the details being given a

dispassionately analytical
treatment, while the heads
of the mourners are crowded
into the top left-hand corner
of the canvas. There is a dismal
sallow colour over everything.
Mantegna takes his attempt
to achieve an insidious, bitter,
implacable design as far
as he can, conceding nothing
to the tonal softness that was
becoming widely adopted in
Venetian painting of the early
sixteenth century.

Giovanni Ambrogio de' Predis

Milan 1455 ca-after 1508

⓭ *Portrait of a Young Man*

oil on panel, 49 × 39 cm

The Portrait of a Young Man, with its sharply defined lighting, has been directly influenced by the precepts and style of Leonardo da Vinci, who almost immediately on settling in Milan established a solid and fruitful friendship with the de' Predis brothers. The Latin maxim, "Life is long if you know how to use it," comes from Seneca, but is also quoted by Leonardo in the *Codex Trivultianus.*

**Master of the Sforza
Altarpiece**

active in Lombardy
1490-1520

14 *The Sforza Altarpiece*

tempera and oil on panel,
230 × 165 cm

Painted by an anonymous
Lombard master around 1494,
and originally in the Milanese
church of Sant'Ambrogio ad
Nemus, this altarpiece is an
impressive and characteristic
example of what was fashionable
at the time of Ludovico il Moro.
The duke and his family, seen
in profile rigidly kneeling, have
been placed in the luxurious
court of the Madonna, in the

presence of four Doctors
of the Church. Everyone
and everything is covered
in an abundance of gold, of
precious mantles, of glittering
jewels, of luxurious ornaments,
to the extent that it is difficult
to see the references to Leonardo
(in the face of the Madonna,
in the sturdy curly-haired
Child, and in the expression
of the left-hand angel).

Donato Bramante

Monte Asdruvaldo, Urbino
1444 - Rome 1514

15 *Christ at the Column*

oil and tempera on panel,
93.7 × 62.5 cm
(in storage from the
Chiaravalle Abbey)

Probably executed for the
Chiaravalle Abbey, this major
painting reveals the amount
of work Bramante carried
out on perspective and on
the volumetric construction
of the human body. The
stunning "Lombard" landscape in the
background and the careful
rendering of the light on Christ's
hair can be attributed to his
study of Leonardo's early

Milanese period. The powerful
emotional expression is
combined with the perfectly
modelled figure, pillar, and
window open onto the landscape.

Bramantino
(Bartolomeo Suardi)

Milan 1465 ca-1530

16 *Crucifixion*

oil on canvas, 372 × 270 cm

Bramantino is one of the most unusual painters of the early sixteenth century, and this *Crucifixion*, the date and original home of which is unknown, is a good example of his own very individual style. Full as it is of symbols, arcane signs and disconcerting architecture this painting is one of the high points of Bramantino's maturity. The figures wrapped in full robes, seem frozen in fixed attitudes and positions (very different from Leonardo's studies in the representation of movement and emotion that were also undertaken in Milan in the same period). The skull, which gives its name to Golgotha, is starkly apparent at the foot of the cross; in the sky are the angel and the devil who exhort and tempt Christ, and above them the sun and the moon are weeping faces.

Raphael (Raffaello Sanzio)

Urbino 1483 - Rome 1520

17 *The Marriage of the Virgin*

oil on panel, 170 × 118 cm
signed and dated on the temple:
"RAPHAEL VRBINAS/MDIIII"

This small altarpiece from the
church of San Francesco in Città
di Castello represents the peak

of Raphael's early years. While
openly paying homage to Perugino
in this painting, the twenty-one-
year old painter also clearly
shows that he has outstripped
his master's models, which seem
a bit tired by comparison. The
scene unfolds in front of the large
temple and fades away into a
distant landscape of hills, fields
and woods, while the eye is drawn
back to the light-filled area of the

open double door at the centre
of the temple. In this harmony
between architecture and natural
world, the figures are arranged
almost casually and quite simply
in a carefully planned series of
semi-circles, which seem to echo
the form of the cupola and the
painting itself. An air of
suspended grace hovers over
the scene, combined with a vague
atmosphere of poetic melancholy.

Francesco Francia
(Francesco Raibolini)
Bologna 1450 ca-1517

18 *The Annunciation*

tempera and oil on panel
transferred to canvas, 237 × 227 cm

This elegant composition was
carried out by Francesco Francia
in 1505 for the church
of San Francesco in Mantua.
The contrast between this
gentle willowy interpretation
of Perugino's style and the hard
graphic impact of the *Dead
Christ* by Mantegna is stunning
considering they were both
painted at the same time,
probably in the same year, and
in the same city of Mantua. Here
Francesco Francia has applied
the Umbrian and Tuscan models,
which had become almost
de rigeur in Italian painting
between the fifteenth and
sixteenth centuries, with such
ease and simplicity. The ordered
arrangement of the figures
and architectural elements
is exemplary, while in the
background the landscape
dissolves into the light-filled
distance.

Gentile Bellini
Venice 1429-1507

Giovanni Bellini
Venice 1430 ca-1516

⑲ *Saint Mark Preaching in Alexandria*

oil on canvas, 347 × 770 cm

Destined for the Scuola Grande di San Marco in Venice, this painting could be said to represent the high point in the genre of narrative *teleri*. It is one of the Brera collections' largest works of art and one of the richest in iconographical elements. It was started by Gentile Bellini in 1504 and after his death (1507) was finished by his brother Giovanni who rendered the buildings framing the setting in a simpler and more monumental manner, concentrating more on the light falling on the scene and emphasizing the figure of Saint Mark who is speaking to the people of Alexandria in Egypt. The scene is organized as if on a theatrical stage: a crowd, in the

centre of which the group of
white-veiled Arab women can
be seen, has gathered to listen
to the words of Saint Mark,
who stands on a dais shaped like
a small bridge. In spite of all
the exotic detail scattered
everywhere, the background
to this wonderful scenography
is obviously based on Piazza
San Marco, while the noble

stature of the oriental dignitaries
seems to be an involuntary
avowal of Ottoman power, which
Gentile Bellini had experienced
at first hand on a diplomatic
mission to Constantinople.

Bernardino Luini

Dumenza near Luino, Varese,
1480 ca - Milan 1532

20 *Vergin of the Rose Garden*

oil on panel, 70 × 63 cm

Dating from between 1508
and 1510, this painting
represents the finest work
of the early part of Bernardino
Luini's career. The Pinacoteca
has quite a number of his
paintings, although lack of space
in the current organization
does not allow for the cycle
of frescoes removed by Luini
to be displayed in the museum.
That he was directly influenced
by Leonardo is clear in the faces

and expressions of the Madonna
and Child. However, the
influence is softened by the
delicate rendering of the light
and colours, while the setting
in a rose garden is based
on the traditional iconography
of the *hortus conclusus*.

Giovanni Bellini
Venice 1430 ca-1516

21 *Madonna and Child*

oil on panel transferred
to canvas, 85 × 118 cm
signed and dated on the left-hand
altar: "JOANNES/BELLINVS/MDX"

The beautifully delicate
light-suffused Venetian landscape
unfolds tranquilly behind the

figures of the Madonna and Child.
Giovanni Bellini was nearly eighty
years old and approaching the end
of a long career when he painted
this memorable composition.
A comparison with the other
paintings by Giovanni Bellini
held by the Pinacoteca di Brera
shows how the painter's style
evolved and in turn influenced
the development of Venetian
painting in the early Renaissance.
In particular, in this 1510

Madonna Bellini can be said
to have created the atmosphere,
natural light, airiness and
luminosity he strove for. The
figures and landscape emerge
effortlessly from the canvas,
the effect being created by using
varying tones of colour around
the figures (look at the faces and
hands for example). The black
outline is no longer visible, since
the drawing has been almost
completely done away with.

Vittore Carpaccio
Venice 1460 ca-1525/1526

22 *Saint Stephen's Dispute with the Doctors of the Sanhedrin*

oil on canvas, 147 × 172 cm
signed and dated in the pedestals
of the two columns, on the left:
"VICTOR/CARPATHIVS/PINXIT;"
on the right: "M/D.XIIII"

Of the three works by Carpaccio
in the Brera, the one that stands
out is *Saint Stephen's Dispute*
(1514). It belongs to
a series of scenes painted
by Carpaccio for the Scuola
dei Lanieri (Confraternity of wool
workers) in Venice, now dispersed
in various museums of the world.
Without detracting from his
characteristic powers of fantastical
narration, Carpaccio has in this

panel achieved stunning clarity
of light and outline, his brilliant
vision supported by an excellent
sense of space, in a fascinating
mix of exoticism provided by the
buildings in the background, the
wise-looking Orientals with whom
Saint Stephen is involved in
animated discussion, and realism
in the portraits of the members
of the confraternity, in long red
and black robes.

34

Giovan Battista Cima
da Conegliano

Conegliano, Treviso,
1459/1460-1517/1518

23 *Saint Peter Enthroned with*
Saints John the Baptist
and Paul

oil on panel transferred
to canvas, 155 × 146 cm

This is one of Cima
da Conegliano's last works;
it came from the refectory
of the Franciscan convent
in Conegliano. It has the
compositional regularity,
symmetry and sense of calm that
is characteristic of this Venetian
artist's work. The details
executed with minute precision
are bathed in a crystal-clear fixed
light that exalts both the striking

design and the brilliance
of the colours. The architectural
details of Saint Peter's throne
and the pilasters at the sides
also underline how strong his ties
still were to late fifteenth century
Venetian culture.

Correggio
(Antonio Allegri)

Correggio, Reggio Emilia,
1489-1534

24 *Nativity with Saint Elizabeth
and the Infant Saint John*

oil on canvas, 79 × 100 cm

An overview of the different
Emilian schools of the
Renaissance, of which Brera
has a remarkable collection,
would not be complete without
the two early exquisite works
by Correggio, the great artist
from Parma who developed
his own alternative versions
of sixteenth-century style.
The two works in the Pinacoteca,
both dating from before 1518,

offer valuable proof of the
development of a separate
individual style. The *Nativity*
(or more accurately the *Adoration
of the Child*), in mainly dark
tones, shows his early training
with the school of Mantegna
which had already been
combined to good effect
with Leonardesque influences.

Girolamo Genga

Urbino 1476 ca-1551

㉕ *Dispute about the
Immaculate Conception*

oil on panel, 438 × 290 cm

This work was the central panel
of a group of paintings carried
out between 1516 and 1518
for the church of the Agostinians
in Cesena. The enormous panel
is one of the most outstanding
works by Girolamo Genga, a
versatile artist from the Marche,
who also turned his hand to
architecture and scenography.
Here we can see that Genga was
well aware of the new figurative

ideas of the early Cinquecento,
from Leonardo's to Raphael's.
He combined them in a most
original way, sometimes
introducing dissonant or bizarre
elements, which places him
firmly among the "eccentrics"
in Italian art of the Renaissance.

Jan de Beer

Antwerp? 1475 - after 1520

26 *Adoration of the Magi;
Nativity; Resting
on the Flight into Egypt*

oil on panel
central panel 156 × 123 cm;
left-hand panel 159 × 58 cm;
right-hand panel 157 × 57 cm

Eclectic and curiously enlivened
by Italianate and classical
allusions, this fine triptych was

painted in Venice (1515–17)
by Jan de Beer. Originally
attributed to Dürer, especially the
central panel with the *Adoration
of the Magi* shows an unusual
proliferation of descriptive detail,
characters and minutely defined
precious materials. The work

is a fine example of the complex
and fascinating period of
transition between the Flemish
tradition and Italian art
of the Renaissance. The city
of Antwerp, which was one of the
main trading and cultural centres
of north-central Europe, was

ideally placed for such
experiments.

Gian Gerolamo Savoldo

Brescia? 1480 ca - Venice?
after 1548

27 *Madonna and Child in Glory with Angels, Saint Peter, Saint Dominic, Saint Paul and Saint Jerome*

oil on panel, 475 × 307 cm
signed bottom right:

"Opera da Jonone Jeronimo
de Brisia di Savoldj"

This altarpiece, commissioned
by the Dominican Order of Pesaro
in 1524, is key to understanding
the stylistic development and
chronology of Savoldo's work.
Although born and trained in
Brescia, Venice became his
adopted home. His work typically
combined plain, unadorned

compact Lombard realism with
rich Venetian colour. Careful study
of Titian's work is also apparent
(the halo of light around the
Madonna closely resembles the
Frari *Assumption*), and has been
further embellished by Savoldo's
typical delicacy in the luminous
rendering of the folds of the
robes. The landscape that
opens up in the centre, is also
noteworthy for the depth of field.

Lorenzo Lotto

Venice 1480 ca -
Loreto, Ancona, 1556

28 *Portrait of Laura da Pola*

oil on canvas, 90 × 75 cm
signed bottom right:
"Laurent.Loto.p."

A work of Lorenzo Lotto's mature
years (ca 1544), this portrait
makes a pair with one of the
husband, Febo da Brescia.
This touching episode in Lotto's
career marks his last contact with
Lombard patrons after a lengthy
sojourn in Bergamo (1513–25).
While there is a general air
of peaceful domesticity in this
portrait of Laura da Pola, a vague
sense of frustration, limited

horizons, also seems to creep
in. In his profound acceptance
of his subjects, in the intensity
of feeling that he transmits,
the emotion that shows through
in his subjects' expressions,
Lotto proved himself a masterful
interpreter of psychological
drama throughout his long
and difficult career.

Paris Bordon

Treviso 1500 ca - Venice 1571

㉙ *Holy Family with Saint Ambrose and Donor*

oil on panel, 93 × 130 cm

This is a typical example of a painting for private devotion. Dating from approximately 1526, it is also an elegant example of the style of Paris Bordon. The scene is fluid with a continuous interweaving of gestures, looks and robes among the five figures. But the elegant composition looks perfectly natural as a result of the brilliant play of light and colours, set in the open air in keeping with the ideas of Giorgione. Although not a very large painting, it truly is the early masterpiece of Paris Bordon's, an accolade that is confirmed by the features, in particular the expressive portrait of the anonymous votary.

Titian (Tiziano Vecellio)

Pieve di Cadore, Belluno,
1488/1490 - Venice 1576

30 *Portrait of Count
Antonio Porcia*

oil on canvas, 115 × 93 cm
signed on the window ledge
on the right: "TITIANVS"

In the heart of the section
on Renaissance Venetian painting
in the Pinacoteca di Brera there
is a small but carefully selected
gallery of the faces, attitudes
and customs that illustrate the
characteristics of the main
Venetian portraitists. The energy
and talent of Titian is everywhere
in evidence. In this guide he is
represented by the *Portrait of
Count Antonio Porcia*, which

he painted in later life in
approximately 1540. Although
it is a relatively simple work
painted in carefully balanced
dark tones, the portrait expresses
the incomparable vitality that
is to be found in all Titian's
works. The young aristocrat,
with dignified calm elegance,
turns on us a brief dazzling
look of formidable energy
and confidence.

Bonifacio Veronese
(Bonifazio de' Pitati)
Verona 1487 ca - Venice 1553

31 *Moses Rescued*
from the Water

oil on canvas, 175 × 345 cm

Bonifacio Veronese belongs
without a doubt to the Venetian
school of the early Cinquecento
and this is one of his most
brilliant enjoyable works
(1540–45). The subject of Moses
rescued from the water was much
loved by painters of the sixteenth
and seventeenth centuries since
it gave them the opportunity
to recount a biblical story in a
non-religious and decorative way.
Bonifacio Veronese goes further
and depicts a merry outing
of beautiful women and young
knights, that looks more like a
courtly diversion. The discovery
of Moses is so obviously a pretext
for the wonderful images of dogs,
clowns, players, and hunters
eating bread and salame.

Gaudenzio Ferrari
Valduggia, Vercelli,
1480 ca - Milan 1546

32 *Martyrdom*
of Saint Catherine

oil on panel, 334 × 210 cm

Brera has a substantial number
of works by Gaudenzio Ferrari,
almost all belonging to the final
stages of his career when, after
1540, Ferrari moved to Milan.
The spectacular altarpiece, in
which he illustrates the moment
preceding the miraculous
shattering of the wheels in
Saint Catherine's martyrdom
comes from the Franciscan
church of Sant'Angelo in Milan.
With his typical overpowering
sense of reality, Gaudenzio
depicts the efforts of the vigorous
executioners and the fear
provoked by the arrival of the
angel with unsheathed sword:
this terrifying popular but
concrete prospect balances the
complex composition with figures
arranged in different planes
at different heights and depths.

45

Tintoretto (Jacopo Robusti)

Venice 1519-1594

33 *The Discovery of the Body of Saint Mark*

oil on canvas, 396 × 400 cm

This scene is part of a cycle that once hung in the Scuola Grande di San Marco in Venice. It depicts with great visionary intensity and theatrical perspective the final episode in the search for the relics of Saint Mark. The ghost of the saint suddenly appears (on the left) to the Venetians who are searching by night among the corpses buried in a church for the remains of their patron. With an imperious gesture Saint Mark tells them to stop looking. At his feet, in an extraordinary example of foreshortening, is a livid naked body lying on a carpet. In the centre is the man who commissioned the work, Tommaso Rangone, wrapped in a golden cloak. The grandiose monumental proportions of the figures, the daring asymmetry of the groups of people within a deeply sloping area, and the flickering lights in the mysterious night, all combine to make this one of the freest and most fascinating of Venetian paintings in the high Renaissance.

Giovan Battista Moroni

Albino, Bergamo,
1520/1524 ca - 1578

34 *Portrait of Antonio Navagero*

oil on canvas, 115 × 90 cm
dated on plinth bottom right:
"M.D.LXV"

The straightforward
likeableness of this character
is confirmation of Moroni's
skill. He was a major exponent
of Renaissance painting
in Bergamo. Using the work
of Lotto and Titian as his
example, Moroni developed
his own style which makes
him one of the most interesting
portraitists of the Cinquecento.
The simple genuine humanity
of the lesser nobility or the
provincial bourgeoisie,
the polite and pleasant
communicativeness of men
and women seen in everyday
surroundings, and the sense
of good-natured satisfaction
(sometimes overshadowed
by religious preoccupations)
all go to make Moroni's
subjects appear lively
and sincere.

Jacopo Bassano
(Jacopo da Ponte)

Bassano, Vicenza,
1510 ca-1592

35 *Saint Roch Visits
the Plague Victims*

oil on canvas, 350 × 210 cm
signed bottom right:
"Jac^s A POTE/BASSIS/PINGEBAT"

Probably created as a votive
altarpiece in the time of the
plague in 1576, the painting
comes from the church of
San Rocco in Vicenza. The
intercession of the Virgin in the
upper part, would appear to be
linked to the strictly devotional
requirements, while the realistic,
even macabre scene of the saint
comforting the plague victims is
a proof of the vigorous popular
realism that underpins all the
work produced by Jacopo and his
family workshop. Nevertheless,
alongside this dramatic sense of
reality, the "provincial" narrative
vein is sustained by thorough
knowledge of the recent
developments in Mannerism, as
can be seen from the perspective
view of the buildings at the lower
end of the canvas.

Veronese (Paolo Caliari)

Verona 1528 - Venice 1588

36 *Baptism and Temptation
of Christ*

oil on canvas, 248 × 450 cm

Among the many important
works by Paolo Veronese
in the Pinacoteca di Brera
we have chosen this vast canvas
executed in his later years
(circa 1582), not only for the
swirling beauty of the group
of angels but also for the very
special subject. The unusual
scene in which even the
landscape seems to be divided
into two distinct parts,
comprises two separate
episodes from the Gospels,
the baptism and the temptation
of Jesus. While in the main part
of the canvas the baptism in
the River Jordan is depicted in
the depths of a wood enlivened
by the flight of angels, on the
right of the canvas is depicted
Christ's encounter with the
Devil, who is holding out the
stone for Christ to transform
into bread.

Federico Barocci
Urbino 1528-1612

37 *Martyrdom of Saint Vitalis*

oil on canvas, 302 × 268 cm
signed and dated bottom right:
"FEDERICVS BAROCIVS/VRBINAS
P.A.D. M.DLXXXIII"

Coming as it does between
the late Renaissance and the
emerging style of the seventeenth
century, this painting by Federico
Barocci (1583, previously in the
church of San Vitale in Ravenna)
clearly marks a profound change
in the history of art. The extreme
and intellectual elegance of
Mannerism is replaced by an
explicit, direct, natural image
with strong popular attraction.
According to the directions of the
Council of Trent for sacred art,
the task of painters was to
illustrate episodes and figures as
clearly as possible so that the
faithful could identify with the
scene (by depicting everyday
objects and people wearing
contemporary clothes).

Vincenzo Campi
Cremona 1536-1591

38 *Fruit Seller*

oil on canvas, 143 × 213 cm

This canvas is part of a cycle
of four compositions, dating
from approximately 1590
and recently reunited under
the Brera roof. In addition
to the fruit seller, there is a
fishwife, a poultry seller and
a kitchen. They are works of
great importance being early
examples of still life. Influenced
by Flemish style of the late
sixteenth century, Vincenzo
Campi has taken the sellers
of a variety of food products
as his "narrative" thread
to present us with a virtuoso
display of different kinds of
fruit, slippery fish, feathered
creatures or pewter dinnerware,
imitating nature to great effect.

Annibale Carracci

Bologna 1560 - Rome 1609

39 *The Samaritan at the Well*

oil on canvas, 170 × 225 cm

Towards 1593, the three Carraccis (the brothers Agostino and Annibale and their cousin Ludovico) painted three works of similar size and evangelic subject, Christ's meetings with women, for the Palazzo Sampieri in Bologna. A comparison of the three works, all housed in Brera, sheds much light on the stylistic similarities and differences of the three Carraccis. Annibale's splendid Samaritan woman is rightly considered a perfect example of Bolognese style: soft fluidity of movement, harmonious expressions, classically noble poses, an eloquence of gesture, and colours influenced by the Venetian tradition.

Guido Reni
Bologna 1575-1642

40 *Saints Peter and Paul*

oil on canvas, 197 × 140 cm

This fine work, painted in Rome in approximately 1605, shows the effective mediation between the calm classicism of Carracci's school and Caravaggio's realism with *chiaroscuro*. The rich dense colours are once again the legacy of the Venetian school, while the clever balancing of gestures and volumes is one of the constant features of Guido Reni's art.

Worthy of note is the original frame with carvings of leaping greyhounds.

Caravaggio (Michelangelo Merisi)

Milan 1571 - Porto Ercole, Grosseto, 1610

41 *Supper at Emmaus*

oil on canvas, 141 × 175 cm

The *Supper at Emmaus*, painted in 1606, belongs to a very delicate moment in Caravaggio's career, but also marks an important change in his painting. He has reduced the descriptive and still-life details to a minimum—details which he had abounded in his earlier works—concentrating his incomparable energy on the faces and emotions of the figures, in a tightly organized sequence of deep shadow and light. Christ's face, half of which has courageously been left in shadow, expresses a feeling of overpowering melancholy: according to the account in the Gospels, the disciples of Emmaus recognize the risen Christ only when he blesses the bread, but at that same moment Jesus disappears from sight. Caravaggio really brings to life this mysterious subtle play on appearance and disappearance, of recognition and abandon, using purely technical but highly sophisticated means. Take for example the virtuoso rendering of the jug on the right, a piece of masterful craftsmanship added to the scene without the slightest trace of exhibitionism.

Orazio Gentileschi
Pisa 1563 - London 1639

42 *The Martyrs Valerian, Tiburtius and Cecilia Visited by an Angel*

oil on canvas, 350 × 218 cm
signed on the base of the organ: "HORATIVS GENTILESC (...) FLORENTINVS FECIT"

This great imposing painting by Orazio Gentileschi is a splendid example of some of Caravaggio's hallmarks combined with striking formal elegance and painstakingly realized details. This rather obscure episode commemorates the matrimony between the christian Cecilia and the pagan Valerian: the appearance of an angel with a crown of flowers indicates the union of the two young people, the conversion to Christianity of Valerian and his brother Tiburtius (in the background) and at the same time foretells their imminent martyrdom, symbolized by the palm carried by the angel; the organ is the traditional attribute of Saint Cecilia, patron saint of musicians.

**Morazzone
(Pier Francesco Mazzucchelli)**

Morazzone, Varese,
1573-before 1626

**Cerano
(Giovanni Battista Crespi)**

Cerano?, Novara, 1575 ca -
Milan 1632

Giulio Cesare Procaccini

Bologna 1574 - Milan 1625

43 *Martyrdom of Saints
Rufina and Seconda
("Picture by Three Hands")*

oil on canvas, 192 × 192 cm

Cardinal Monte who was an
important collector and patron in
early seventeenth-century Milan
supported this strange project
which gave interesting if far from
homogeneous results.
The three best Lombard painters
of the seventeenth century were
invited to work on the same
canvas for purposes of
comparison. By examining a
single painting (or indeed by
simply comparing the three
angels) some of the stylistic
features of the three major
painters of the time could be

identified. The dramatic and
sculptural Cerano painted
the left side of the canvas
with the knight, the decapitated
saint on the ground and the
unhappy little angel who is
hugging a dog. The Bolognese
origin of Giulio Cesare Procaccini
is apparent in the supple
elegance and delicate complexion
of the saint who awaits her
martyrdom comforted by the
angel. Morazzone, theatrical
and imaginative, saw to the
overall composition of the
painting with light that catches
the dark executioner and
the delicate angel in flight.

In the banner at the top of the painting: PANEM ANGELORVM MANDVCAVIT HOMO

Daniele Crespi

Busto Arsizio, Varese,
1597/1600 - Milan 1630

44 *The Last Supper*

oil on canvas, 335 × 220 cm

Based on an idea of Gaudenzio
Ferrari's, Daniele Crespi
has arranged the *Last Supper*
on a vertical orientation. Christ
and the apostles are squashed
in around a relatively small table
that is almost completely covered
in large plates of food.
The compositional structure
is thus very different from the
almost obligatory prototype of
Leonardo's *Last Supper*, which
the painter nonetheless obviously
is very well acquainted with,
since he has taken from it the
animation of the figures and
even some of the faces. This
work came to the Pinacoteca
from a convent of Benedictine
nuns in Brianza and is one
of the most important works
of the painter who was to become
an eminent victim of the plague
of 1630.

Bernardo Strozzi

Genoa 1581 - Venice 1644

45 *Portrait of a Knight of Malta*

oil on canvas, 129 × 98 cm

The work of the Ligurian seventeenth-century painters are conveniently hung in the same room as the Flemish masters so that direct parallels may be drawn. Among the principal painters of the Genoese school is Bernardo Strozzi. His marvellous *Portrait of a Knight of Malta* (1629 ca) arouses such admiration that

a comparison with Van Dyck automatically springs to mind. Strozzi's brushstrokes are rich and soft, reminiscent of Rubens; they are enlivened by saturated vivid colours. His taste in colour has definite Venetian leanings and in fact Strozzi moved to Venice for the last fifteen years of his life.

Pieter Paul Rubens

Siegen 1577 - Antwerp 1640

46 *The Last Supper*

oil on panel, 304 × 250 cm

Along with a large number of works of the seventeenth century Flemish and Dutch schools, this vast canvas came to Brera as a result of an exchange of works with the Louvre in 1812. It is a mature work by Rubens, painted in collaboration with his workshop between 1630 and 1632 for the cathedral of Malines. Although only partly his work, the painting shows Rubens' ability to rework different influences (Titian, Caravaggio, Veronese) into a completely new style that with its generous sweep draws the viewer into the painting on a wave of colour, gestures and drapery. The school of Rubens, comprising in certain periods over one-hundred pupils, was highly characteristic of the development of Flemish painting in the first half of the seventeenth century; it is represented in the Pinacoteca di Brera by works by Jordaens, Van Dyck, Snyders, Jan Bruegel the Elder and Jan Fyt.

Anton van Dyck

Antwerp 1599 - London 1641

47 *Portrait of a Noblewoman*

oil on canvas, 140 × 107 cm

This noblewoman, refined and severe in her sober mourning dress, which is in stark contrast to the blaze of jewels she is wearing, is no longer thought to be the Princess Amelia of Solms, wife of the governor of the Netherlands, but is more likely to be a member of the du Croy family of Brussels. Painted in circa 1635, the painting belongs to Van Dyck's late period.

It confirms once again his absolute mastery of the baroque portrait: although the tones are subdued, based on the black clothes she is wearing, the work highlights the delicacy of the hands and face of the still young widow, while the golden yellow curtain on the left adds a note of luxuriousness to the composition.

Pietro da Cortona (Pietro Berrettini)

Cortona, Arezzo,
1596 - Rome 1669

48 *Madonna and Child with Saints John the Baptist, Felix da Cantalice, Andrew and Catherine*

oil on canvas, 296 × 205 cm
signed bottom centre:
"PETRVS BERETINVS CORTON.^{SIS} F"

This wonderful example of a baroque altarpiece dates from around 1630 and therefore belongs to the painter's early maturity, when he was already carrying out commissions for the Barberini family. Pietro da Cortona adopts the ordered symmetrical layout of the Renaissance *Sacre Conversazioni*, but with spectacular overtones. Before the colonnaded background, the painter has hung a curtain that has been raised like a stage curtain to reveal the light-filled scene in which Saint Catherine's rich garments have a decidedly theatrical character.

Evaristo Baschenis

Bergamo 1617-1677

49 *Still Life with Musical Instruments*

oil on canvas, 60 × 88 cm
signed on the side of the casket:
"Evaristo Baschenis F."

This memorable masterpiece by Evaristo Baschenis is one of the most important Italian still lifes of the seventeenth century. Musical instruments are Baschenis' favourite subject. Combined with the undeniable skill with which he represents perspective, and his evocation of materials that almost seems an optical illusion, the painter adds a melancholy note of reflection on the passing of time. The depiction of a layer of dust on the instruments lying silent and abandoned is eloquent indeed.

Luca Giordano
Naples 1634-1705

50 *Ecce Homo*

oil on canvas, 158 × 155 cm

Attractive, gifted and unscrupulous, Luca Giordano took his inspiration directly from an engraving by Dürer to create a scene with impressive lighting effects. The painting dates from around 1660, when the Neapolitan painter directly rivalled the style of Mattia Preti. Showing off his proverbial eclecticism, Luca Giordano pulls off a startling unstable composition, full of unusual features, such as the figure wrapped in a cloak that looks phosphorescent.

Giambattista Tiepolo

Venice 1696 - Madrid 1770

51 *The Madonna of the Carmel with Saints Simon Stock, Teresa of Avila, Alberto of Vercelli, the Prophet Elijah and the Souls of Purgatory*

oil on canvas, 210 × 650 cm

This large complex composition was commissioned in 1721 by the confraternita del Suffragio (Confraternity of Intercession for the souls of the departed) for the church of Sant'Aponal in Venice, and is one of the most important works of Tiepolo's youth.
The subject is fairly complicated since the main characters and the devotional aspects of the Carmelite order have to be combined in a single dramatic action. In particular, on the two sides of the painting are the episodes where the Virgin hands over the scapular to Saint Simon Stock and the prayer of intercession for the souls in Purgatory. The painting has had quite an eventful history: it was sold at auction in 1865 and then divided into two parts which were put on the art market separately. In 1925, the two halves reappeared on the market, were purchased by the Chiesa family and donated to Brera. The painting was finally put together once more in 1950. On

the left, with the naked bodies of
the souls in Purgatory, Tiepolo's
highly contrasting chiaroscuro
effects are clearly indicative of the
influence
of Piazzetta in particular and the
seventeenth-century tradition in
general. Moving gradually towards
the right of the painting is an
ever more extensive and diffuse
luminosity, combined with solemnly
eloquent gestures and that sparkling
brushwork that was to characterize
Tiepolo's whole career.

Pitocchetto
(Giacomo Ceruti)

Brescia 1698-1767

52 *Boy Seated with a Basket,
Eggs and Chickens*

oil on canvas, 130 × 95 cm

Giacomo Ceruti was born
in Milan but worked mainly
in Brescia. He was the most
committed and best interpreter
of the "painting of reality" in the
eighteenth century. His favourite
subjects were the lowly, the misfits,
the vagabonds, what in Lombard
dialect were known as "pitocchi"
(from *pidocchio*, louse) and thus
Ceruti's nickname of "Pitocchetto."
His paintings of these paupers
are mostly medium to large, with
figures in natural proportions:
in other words they are not small
decorative and inoffensive genre
scenes, but are of characters full
of sorrowful dignity, that "speak"
to us by means of their mute code
of expressions. The boy with
the large baskets (his delicate
features betraying the fact that
he has been forced to work
prematurely) is the protagonist
of a humanity that had had very
few occasions to make itself seen
on the painting scene.

Fra Galgario
(Vittore Ghislandi)

Bergamo 1655-1743

53 *Portrait of a Gentleman*
(Flaminio Tassi?)

oil on canvas, 127 × 98 cm

Although he started painting late
in life (no works of his before
he was forty have been found),
Fra Galgario is one of the most
interesting portraitists of the
eighteenth century in Europe.
He was particularly fond of the
oval format also used for this
portrait of what is probably a
gentleman of the Tassi family
of Bergamo. The figure is shown
from the pelvis and is slightly

twisted to highlight the
exquisitely detailed embroidery
that decorates his jacket.
Fra Galgario varies the
technique used to lay on colour
(smoother and more even
on the face and fluffy curls
of the powdered wig, richer
and denser on his clothes),
thus achieving strikingly
rich effects in a basically
monochrome painting.

67

Canaletto
(Giovanni Antonio Canal)
Venice 1697-1768

54 *View of the Basin of San Marco from the Customs Point*

View of the Grand Canal Looking Towards the Customs Point, from Campo San Vio

oil on canvas, 53 × 70 cm each

These two works in the Pinacoteca di Brera form a famous pair of views of Venice, and mark the beginning of the mature phase of Canaletto's career. Here we can see that Canaletto found his own individual expression as an artist. The colours are paler, the outline is more clear-cut and precise,

the sunlight is at the meridian and diffused, and the "macchiette," the figures that enliven the scene, are ever more numerous and active. The *camera ottica*, the device with lenses that Canaletto employed to study urban views, was used mainly to precisely fix drawings from life, while the painting proper was carried out in the workshop.

68

Bernardo Bellotto
Venice 1720 - Warsaw 1780

55 *View of Villa Melzi
alla Gazzada*

View of Gazzada

oil on canvas,
64.5 × 98.5 cm each

This pair of "portraits of
Lombardy," masterpieces of the
youthful period of Bernardo
Bellotto before his departure for
foreign parts, record the painter's
impressions during a journey in
Northern Italy in 1744. They are
views of the Gazzada property
on Lake Varese, within sight
of Monte Rosa—a very different
setting from the extensive lively
urban scenes of the canals of
Venice. Bellotto paints for us
an image that is both lucid
and enamoured of a landscape,
a season, a time, sensitively
grasping even the slightest
change in light and colour on a
cool morning in early Autumn.

**Giovanni Battista
Piazzetta**

Venice 1683-1754

56 *Rebecca and Eleazar
at the Well*

oil on canvas, 102 × 137 cm

This beautifully executed work,
the quintessential image of the
theatrical and expanded spirit
of Venetian art in the eighteenth
century, belongs to the late phase
of the painter's career.
Following Tiepolo's example,
Piazzetta gradually gave up the
strongly contrasting *chiaroscuro*
effects of the baroque tradition
in favour of a diffuse noon-day
light. The subject of the painting
is biblical (Isaac's offer of
matrimony presented by Eleazar
to the beautiful Rebecca at the
well), but it is treated in a
decidedly non-religious way
with the entertaining addition
of secondary figures and animals.

Pierre Subleyras

Saint-Gilles-du-Gard
1699 - Rome 1749

57 *Crucifixion with Mary
Magdalen and Saints
Eusebius and Philip Neri*

oil on canvas, 408 × 232 cm
signed and dated bottom centre:
"Petrus Subleyras Pinxit
Romae 1744"

This is part of the founding group
of works in the Brera collection.
A work of exemplary noble and
controlled balance the *Crucifixion*
clearly marks a turning point in
the history of art. Having worked
in Rome and achieved success, the
French painter Subleyras suggested
that the theatricality of baroque
painting should be abandoned
in favour of a more rigorously
calculated image that would seem
to herald the later developments
in the art of the Enlightenment
and Neoclassical art.

Anton Raphael Mengs

Aussig, Bohemia,
1728 - Rome 1779

58 *Portrait of the Singer
Domenico Annibali*

oil on canvas, 125 × 95 cm
dated on the base
of the columns: "1750"

As well as being a first-class
intellectual and artist, Mengs
was also one of the leading lights
of European culture in the
transition phase between
the Enlightenment and early
Neoclassicism. This portrait,
dedicated to a famous singer
from the Marche who was feted
in all the courts of Europe, does
however belong to the early years
of the artist's career. There is
a certain pomp and ostentation
in the subject's clothes and
gestures, while his face expresses
an intelligent self confidence.

Andrea Appiani

Milan 1754-1817

59 *Olympus
(Coronation of Jupiter)*

oil on canvas, 45 × 136 cm

This elegant Neoclassical
painting was destined to decorate
a small room of the Palazzo
Reale in Milan, where many
decorative ideas of the
Napoleonic age were developed.
Although painted in 1806 it
was never hung in the place for
which it was designed and after
the fall of Napoleon in 1814, it
remained in the painter's studio.
The tone of the painting is
celebratory (beneath Zeus's big
black beard Napoleon's features
are evident; the eagle is a typical
element in Napoleonic
iconography), and the search
for noble beauty is evident in
every detail of the composition.

Francesco Hayez
Venice 1791 - Milan 1882

60 *The Kiss*

oil on canvas, 112 × 88 cm

This is Hayez's most famous
work: from the time of its
completion in 1859 it became
very well known and is
emblematic of the Italian
nineteenth-century painting. The
exchange of affectionate caresses
binds the two lovers, who seem
to have forgotten all their reserve
with the strength of their passion.
Nevertheless, closer examination,
in particular of the young man's
clothes, reveals that the scene is
not set in the painter's time but
in the Mediaeval period. The
strict conventions that governed
art until the second half of the
nineteenth century dictated that it
was "improper" to have a love
scene set in reality.

Silvestro Lega
Modigliana, Forlì,
1826 - Florence 1895

61 *The Pergola*

oil on canvas, 75 × 93.5 cm
signed and dated bottom left:
"S. Lega 1868"

Lega was a member of the group
of Macchiaioli in Tuscany. He
favoured images that depicted
intimate feelings, pastoral settings,
and serene dialogue. This painting
is an excellent demonstration of
the concept of "macchie" or spots
of light and colour. A dense
pergola protects a group of women
from the heat in the slightly
shimmering almost misty
atmosphere created by the sun
in a summer afternoon. A charming
web of feelings interwoven with
exchanged gestures and glances
is played out against the dappled
light and shade.

Giovanni Fattori

Livorno 1825 - Florence 1908

62 *The Red Wagon (The Rest)*

oil on canvas, 88 × 170 cm
signed bottom left: "Gio. Fattori"

This painting marks a very important phase of Giovanni Fattori's maturity. It was painted in 1887 when the Macchiaioli movement was losing its initial cohesion and Fattori was becoming increasingly interested in pursuing his solitary study of the work of the *butteri* (cowboys), herdsmen and peasants of the Maremma. Here,

during a rest, the enormous outlines of the oxen freed from the shaft and the heavy mass of the *contadino* sitting on the ground are silhouetted against a harsh coastal background. The land below a heavy sultry sky is scorched by the sun, on the edge of a sea that looks leaden in the summer heat.

Giovanni Segantini

Arco, Trent, 1858 -
Schafberg, Engadina, 1899

63 *Spring Pastures*

oil on canvas, 95 × 155 cm
initialled and dated bottom right:
"G.S. 1896"

The search for solitude, purity
and clear air led Segantini
to climb ever higher into
the mountains looking for
that mystical, moral and
environmental atmosphere
that is a feature of the work
of his later years.
This alpine pasture
in Engadina is a splendid
demonstration of the effects
of luminosity achieved with
the technique of Divisionism.
Segantini was aware of the
importance of this painting,
from both the point of view
of technique and the subtley
ambiguous image that is a
combination of alpine reality
and mystic symbolism.

Giuseppe Pellizza da Volpedo

Volpedo, Alessandria,
1868-1907

64 *Fiumana*

oil on canvas, 255 × 438 cm

Painted between 1895 and 1897,
this is the second version of the
Quarto Stato, the most famous
and most abused painting
of a social subject in Italian art,
the final version of which is kept
in the Gallery of Modern Art
in Milan. Pellizza worked on this
scene for ten years in all, proof
of his deep innovative
commitment, both from the point
of view of style, with the adoption
on a large scale, of the technique
of Divisionism, as well as of the
subject matter. A compact group
of workers is marching together
towards us out of the canvas:
a woman carrying a baby
increases the dramatic force
of this declaration of a new
class of workers in Italy which
at that time was undergoing
a painful process of
industrialization.

Umberto Boccioni

Reggio Calabria 1882 -
Verona 1916

65 *Riot in the Galleria*

oil on canvas, 76 × 64 cm
signed top right: "U. BOCCIONI"

Only a few years after the
"bourgeois" urban views of the
late nineteenth century, Boccioni
experimented with this painting
in which, beneath the electric
light, a kind of diabolical dance
takes place. The expression of
the movement, the image of
modern life, the explosive force
of an energy finally liberated, the
rush of progress, the speed of
urban growth, the spread of
electric light and cars are some
of the most typical aspects of
Futurist painting, expressed
either directly or symbolically.
In *Riot in the Galleria* (1911),
Boccioni uses a technique similar
to Divisionism but which seems
to render the colours
incandescent; he describes with
obvious enjoyment and from an
unusual perspective the small
crowd that has gathered around
two women who are squabbling
in front of a café.

Carlo Carrà

Quargnento, Alessandria,
1881 - Milan 1966

66 *The Metaphysical Muse*

oil on canvas, 90 × 66 cm
signed and dated bottom left:
"C. CARRÀ/917"

During the First World War, a
group of artists (de Chirico,

Carrà, Savinio, de Pisis) founded
the Metaphysical movement in
opposition to Futurism. It is
characterized by clearly defined,
precise forms, clear fixed lighting
and geometrical outlines in
mysterious immobility that
renders even more arcane and
enigmatic the encounter between
objects, mannequins, architecture
and overturned perspective.
Metaphysical painting is

represented in the Pinacoteca
by three major works by Carrà,
all from 1917, characterized by
shiny clear colour, assemblies
of heterogeneous objects and the
mute presence of mannequins.
It would seem to be a flight from
reality, although there is no lack
of references to contemporary
events: the map of Istria with
a bull's eye is a direct reference
to the Great War.

Giorgio Morandi
Bologna 1890-1964

67 *Still Life (Great Metaphysical Still Life)*

oil on canvas, 68.5 × 72 cm

Thanks to the donation of Emilio and Maria Jesi, Brera has an exceptional group of works by Giorgio Morandi covering the different phases of his career. Of great importance are his still lifes from the metaphysical period (1918–19) when Morandi, at the beginning of a long, patient and solitary search, outlines with unfailing precision the shapes of simple objects on a neutral background, in silent monochrome. The difference between Morandi's austere compositions with a few everyday objects and very little colour, and Carrà's richer more colourful subjects should be noted.

Pablo Picasso

Málaga 1881 - Mougins 1973

68 *Bull's Head*

oil on canvas, 116 × 89 cm
signed top right: "Picasso;"
dated bottom right: "6.4.42"

This striking work from
the Second World War years
is a remarkable example of the
return to Neo-Cubism launched
by Picasso in the thirties.
The dramatic skull of the bull,
laid on a table cloth and
apparently streaked with blood,
takes on a solemn and tragic
tone of denunciation
of the horrors of the war.

This volume was printed by Elemond S.p.A.
at the plant in Martellago (Venice) in 1999